Young, Catholic, Female.

Why I want to be a priest

Jacqueline Straub

Fisher King Publishing

Young, Catholic, Female.

Copyright © 2017 Jacqueline Straub

Fisher King Publishing Ltd,
The Studio,
Arthington Lane,
Pool in Wharfedale,
LS21 1JZ,
England.

Cover photograph: Meli Straub at www.meli-photodesign.de

Translation to English: Birgitta Bungart and Michael Plümer

A CIP catalogue record of this book is available from the British Library
ISBN 978-1-910406-57-1

www.fisherkingpublishing.co.uk

Contents

Jacqueline Straub

Jacqueline Straub was born in 1990 in Sigmaringen in the south of Germany (Baden-Württemberg). Her path of faith began at the age of fifteen when she was with a school friend at a Christian youth camp. Since then, Jacqueline describes feeling in her heart a calling to become a roman catholic priest.

Through pilgrimages to Rome, Assisi, Taizé and Jerusalem, Jacqueline's faith in God and in the Church, grew and strengthened. Since her first sense of calling to become a priest, she has striven to help develop a new courage in faith and to be a part of an ever-growing movement to reinvigorate the roman catholic Church.

Jacqueline began to study catholic theology in Freiburg im Breisgau (Germany), Fribourg (Switzerland) and Lucerne (Switzerland). In July 2016, she finished her masters in theology with summa cum laude.

Jacqueline founded an online web presence to realize

a modern form of church and Christianity that brings the Christian faith to a younger, wider audience and one that brings the Church in a new way to people through the use of technology such as using video to transmit sermons as well as spiritual texts, articles and commentary on current religious events. Please visit www.preachers.news

Since 2011, Jacqueline has publicly proclaimed her vocation and regularly speaks about it in the media. She was a guest on several TV talk shows across the German speaking area of Europe. See more at www.jacqueline-straub.de

Jacqueline lives in Switzerland and works as a freelance journalist, author and lecturer in the church and on theological issues.

Foreword

Ida Raming
Author, theologian and leading campaigner for women's rights in the church.

"I feel as if I were called to be a fighter, a priest, an apostle, a doctor, a martyr; as if I could never satisfy the needs of my nature without performing, for Your sake, every kind of heroic action at once. I feel as if I'd got the courage to be a Crusader, a Pontifical Zouave, dying on the battlefield in defence of the Church. And at the same time I want to be a priest..."

These are the words of the 'little' Saint Thérèse of Lisieux (1873-1897), pronounced around 125 years ago.

Generations of Christian women, saints-among them, were people who, like Thérèse, felt called to priestly ministry - they were rejected with threadbare, discriminatory answers from men of the church. What degradation, what suffering for the affected women and what missed opportunities and prevented reforms for the church!

The opening of the Second Vatican Council (1962-65) offered for the first time a chance that the voices of several women appointed to the priesthood could become public. In a joint action, they prepared written submissions to Council II. The movement became stronger, not only in Europe, but internationally.

In response to the increasing movement for equality and for women's ordination, the Vatican church leadership, deeply imprisoned in the patriarchy, had only one answer: the doorways for priestesses were all the more relentlessly closed in the post-conciliar phase of the restoration. *(1976: Congregation for the Doctrine of the Faith: Interinsigniores, 1994 : Pope John Paul II: Ordinatio Sacerdotalis).*

The women who had been called, however, did not abandon the task of striving for their vocation, but they were getting older, and the life of the pioneers slowly ended without the patriarchal nuns opening their doors. This is a grave injustice - a godless resistance to a renewal of the Church by the power of the Holy Spirit!

But the divine spirit, the 'spirit of truth,' continued to stir, and does not fail.

Now a young woman, Jacqueline Straub, stands up and speaks out - she is, thankfully, not alone around the world - and boldly confesses to her vocation as a priestess. Although a child is little religious, apart from the traditional rites (for example, First Communion), the participation in a Christian youth camp becomes a turning point, "I felt a wish within me, which was strengthened in that week: I wanted to become a priest in the Roman Catholic church". She felt within her, "that this was my way". At the same time, however, she was aware that her vocation "could not be fulfilled within the Roman Catholic Church".

She embarked on a study of theology and also gains greater understanding about the theological hurdles that oppose the female priesthood, and she deals with it bravely.

Although she had not finished her studies at the time, she spoke out about her call to the priesthood, as well as to fellow human beings, who decisively reject this possibility for women, "I would not be myself, if I did not stand firm for this calling by God". She expressly refuses to conceal her faith, and calls upon other protesting women not to deny the call of God. This is the only way to change the important things in the Church, "It is time to break the silence and to stand up for a renewed church... How can a discrimination against females any longer be legitimized in the name of Jesus Christ?".

Her struggle for the realization of her vocation to the priesthood connects the author with the commitment to a sweeping renewal of the Church. To this end, she makes several proposals; reform of the mind and of the heart: "In order to stay alive the Roman Catholic Church needs a change".

"...the Roman Catholic Church will become attractive again only if and when it manages to reach out to the lives of people through genuine pastoral care, which consists of practical help in everyday life."

The Church must not push anyone into the margins. In dialog with each other and with respect for each other, Straub sees important ways of effectively counteracting exclusion, though without being uncritical, e.g. against neo-fascists, who are clearly opposed to the message of Christ. She also promises, "I will not hesitate or stop when faced with the opposition of reactionary bishops, clergy or laymen...". A direction that deserves the utmost respect.

My express wish for the author and all those expressing such belief, is that their message and their courageous testimony will not remain unheard but lead to the outcome for which we all hope and pray. The disastrous discrimination against women by the Church itself is doing so much damage by preventing the urgently needed renewal of the Church.

With the help of God may the words of Jacqueline Straub be heard and acted upon.

Ida Raming

Chapter One

Journey of Faith

The liturgical year was formative

"I believe"- these are the first two words of the Apostles' Creed, which originated across the third and fourth centuries. I would like to begin with these two forceful words.

Thus I believe that change can be effected without armed force and without hate speech, but solely through a revolution of the heart.

But most of all I believe in God and in the Roman Catholic Church.

Faith in God is not something spectacular, but neither something ordinary in our pluralistic Western world.

My faith has developed at a very slow pace. I attended a Roman Catholic kindergarten. However, I do not have especially positive memories of that period of time. Throughout my schooldays I had religious instruction.

Today I know, that my time in kindergarten and elementary

school has contributed to form me as a Christian.

Most of the pictures I painted during that time contain Christian symbols; fishes, crucifixes and small churches. But there is little good or impressive with respect to content that I can remember.

In my family, Christian faith did not play a role. Although daily life was determined by the feast days of the Roman Catholic liturgical year, this did not have much influence on my religious education. As far as I can remember, saying grace and evening prayer were not practiced in my family.

In my childhood I visited several churches, but not in order to attend divine service on Sundays. No, my uncle was an art historian and took me along to visit churches and monasteries as part of his study. It was he who aroused my early interest in history, art and also in theology. To him I owe my present love for ecclesiastical art.

A step towards community with God: the First Holy Communion

I grew up in a small village. There it was traditional for third-graders to receive their First Holy Communion. Together with four other children I was prepared for the big event in Communion lessons that were taught by a different mother each month. I still remember those lessons very well.

As befitted the theme of this special First Holy Communion

we had an exercise book, which we worked through step by step. Additionally we crafted, painted and baked bread. Moreover, in religious instruction at school we learned a lot about the First Holy Communion and were prepared for the first reconciliation. The latter I fear, because our parish priest was very strict. Nevertheless, at that time I did not really know, why I was supposed to do all that.

Together with my classmates I went to confession on a Friday afternoon. It was agonizing. Afterwards, as a penitence, I prayed three Lord's Prayers as ordered by the parish priest. Greatly relieved I left the church, not because I felt any better after the confession, but because I was glad to have finished my talk with the priest.

To avoid any issues on the day of the First Holy Communion we children, for several weeks, had been rehearsing the entire sequence of the mass with our parish priest. I tried hard to do everything correctly as I did not want to be scolded.

And then finally the time had come. The feast, that was meant to be an important step for me to become a Christian, was very close. As a nine-year-old I was barely aware of this, but I am certain, that in addition to baptism this First Holy Communion that I received on White Sunday of the year 2000 was a cornerstone of my flourishing love to Christ and to His church. This First Holy Communion strengthened my sense of belonging to the church and most of all it strengened my faith in Jesus Christ.

Today I am able to realize, that my First Holy Communion was an important event in my life as a Christian, although at that time I was glad to remove the veil after mass and finally be able to celebrate the festivities together with my family.

Altar girl? No thanks!

It was customary to become an altar girl after the First Holy Communion. But I did not want to do that. My sister had already refused to serve as an altar girl with our parish priest. I followed her lead and shortly realized that this had been the right decision. I kept asking myself: why should I do this to me, to serve with this parish priest week after week when I had already regarded the monthly elementary school masses as hell on earth.

For me there was nothing worse than this one particular Friday every month. I had to sit still for one hour and I was not even allowed to look at the beautiful paintings within the church.

As soon as I lifted my head and directed my eyes at the ceiling, the parish priest loudly hissed my name. As I have mentioned he was very strict. To this day I remember him as a dangerous person, somebody, who would have fit well into a medieval gothic novel.

I have never felt at home in that parish. For that reason I never went to church. Even on Christmas, the only time of the year that our family participated in the service, we went to another parish.

My mother never forced us to go to church. My grandmother often urged me to attend with her. But my sister and I resisted, to a large extent, successfully.

A few times I attended mass with my Grandma. We would sit in the last row, even behind the actual pews. And I did not understand anything of what happened. I was not even allowed to browse through the hymnbook and again I was condemned to sit still. How glad I was when this one hour was over and I was released once again into freedom. These few hours that I spent in mass were easily the longest and most unpleasant times of my childhood.

All my classmates became altar servers, whether they wanted to or not. As I was the only one in our entire class who did not serve with the parish priest at the altar, I had to suffer the mockery of the other children. But soon, as they themselves grew not to like the service they were forced to undertake, they stopped taunting me. Nevertheless, they had to continue attending.

If I had become an altar girl with this parish priest, I would have left the church in frustration at twelve years of age, as it was customary in our parish. From then on I would have given the church the cold shoulder. Highly likley I would not have attended mass again and I would not have come to know the diversity of the Roman Catholic Church.

I am glad that I became an altar girl only when I had come

of age. Then I could serve with conviction.

Faith in God? I don't know...

My grandmother was a very pious woman. She prayed the rosary daily, attended mass on Sundays, and she regularly read the Bible. That did not really impress me much as a child. For me God did not play an extraordinarily big role. I just muddled along and looked forward to Advent season and the days of Easter. I, like many other children, had been baptized and had participated in the First Holy Communion, but besides that I did not care much for the church. I liked religious instruction at school well enough; I was attentive as in every other subject and achieved good grades, but it did not appear convincing to me during that time.

While I was at secondary school, a divine service was held at the beginning and at the end of a school year. Until eighth grade I used to play truant on these occasions. I did not see any reason to sit still in a church again. In my eyes that would have been wasted time. For me divine service was dispensible, and I preferred to spend the time taking a stroll through town with my friends.

The Decision
The Christian youth camp

Due to our move to a small town I got into a parish, which later became my spiritual home. The move to a new town meant a move to a new school. There I met my first boyfriend and my then best friend, who also was new in the same class. To those two I owe my Christian faith.

Within a brief period of time I had met two people who were already Christians of conviction and were both members of Christian communities. My friend belonged to a free church, my boyfriend to the Roman Catholic church. Both opened a new world to me, a world with God. During the first year in my new home town I attended mass at the Catholic church several times with my boyfriend. There I experienced something that was new to me; a parish priest who could move people by his sermon. I got a message out of these masses, one that made me think about God.

I talked a lot with my friend about her strong faith and about my own slowly budding faith. During this time I listened to many new spiritual songs and to 'Jesus-songs'. These lively songs were some of my earliest points of contact with God. I bought a small Bible and began to browse through it. With the mother of my boyfriend I often talked about God and the church. However, my own deep faith in God grew in a free church summer camp. I had already felt something inside me, but could not exactly put it into words. Then for one week during the summer holidays I went, together with my friend, to a Christian youth camp. Young people had come from all over Germany and had set up camp on a large meadow.

Several times per day we would meet for prayer in a big tent. Otherwise we would come together in smaller groups, where we took our meals and participated in events.

I can still remember the first time I was asked to say grace. It was a special moment for me as it is for anyone at the table who would be asked. I recall how the leader of the group told me that I would surely make a good pastor.

During the daily workshops and during the evening program one could get to know the other participitants better and talk to them about God.

I loved the prayer times in the big tent. We sang modern songs in German and English and thus celebrated God in a totally different way compared to what I knew from the Roman Catholic church.

These were vivid songs, accompanied by electric guitar and percussion. The lyrics of the songs were projected to a large screen. We danced happily to the music, some leaping through the tent and raising their arms to the sky in thanks to God for this special moment.

The speeches, prayers and sermons were lively and very close to us young people. I felt something incredible during these prayer times. It seemed that everybody in that tent had the sense of the presence of God. We just felt Him.

During this week I talked often with young people who, for a long time, had already enjoyed a strong relationship with God. To get to the bottom of the incredibly beautiful feeling inside me, I often retreated after prayer times, read the Bible and prayed a lot. During those days of celebrating together and of intense prayer my heart began to burn.

I experienced something that even today I cannot put into words. I felt a wish within me, which was strengthened in that week: I wanted to become a priest in the Roman Catholic Church. In this week I experienced something profound that told me, this was my way.

However, I was aware of the fact that this career aspiration, could not be fulfilled within the Roman Catholic Church, at least not at present. Nevertheless, I knew that the months I had spent with my new friends in my new home town had triggered something that changed me deeply. I knew, I belonged to God and He had sent me on my way.

The Confirmation

My friend and I often attended divine service together, and from the beginning I was excited about the town priest. I can still remember the first time we went to church together. I hardly knew the liturgical service. So my friend and his mother explained to me the individual gestures, positions and prayers as they would have explained it to a child preparing for the First Holy Communion. As it was customary to receive confirmation at the age of fifteen or sixteen years in this parish, I decided to receive confirmation together with my friend in the parish of this very friendly priest.

In my former parish I would not have been inclined to receive confirmation. But now I felt that this was the right decision. I was determined to deepen my relationship with God. I used the time of preparing for confirmation to amplify my faith. Thus I experienced more and more urgently my wish to become a female Catholic priest.

For me the confirmation meant a big step toward complete belonging to the community of faith, and at the same time a giant personal step towards God. My relationship with God was taking shape.

I deepened my faith through prayer and reading the Bible, through conversation with the confirmation catechists and the parish priest.

My confirmation was a special moment and I felt the Holy Spirit flow over us confirmands. I was literally being inspired. I still attended divine services after my confirmation.

The decision to become an altar server took a little bit longer, although, again and again, I thought that I wanted to serve at the altar with that parish priest. But I thought it strange to become an altar server considering my age. However, my wish to be as close as possible to the eucharist grew stronger and stronger. It was no longer sufficient for me to 'merely' sit in a pew. I felt a desire to also wear a white, flowing alb.

One and a half years after my confirmation - I was seventeen years old then - I took all my courage and, after lengthy consideration decided to become an altar server.

Altar girl? Yes please!

The parish priest, at whose church I had received confirmation, and to whom I strongly owed the deepening of my faith, was appointed to a higher position. His successor was a priest who would have a lasting effect on me and who would accompany me on my road to faith. I decided to approach him and propose to serve as an altar girl. He was very pleased and allowed me to serve without further preparation. The parish priest knew that I would always attend mass on Sundays and that I knew the liturgical service by that time. Nevertheless, there was a difference between being a 'quiet observer' in the pew, and taking an active part in divine service. I quickly learned the various tasks of the service and loved them so much that I did not serve only once a week, but whenever there was a need. I took my service as an altar girl very seriously.

Through serving at the altar my love of the church and my wish to celebrate mass myself later in life grew ever stronger. My pastor felt this and talked to me about it a lot. The pastoral assistant, who would later be my teacher of religious instruction at school, always supported me as well. It was he who advised me to study theology. I believe that, each Sunday, my wish to become a priest grew more intense.

The parish became my family and thus I became a group leader and then supervised younger altar servers each week. Until the start of my studies of theology at university, I was active both in the parish and beyond. The parish organized a number of pilgrimages for altar servers, to Rome, to Taizé and to Assisi, to name just a few destinations. On each successive journey I felt a stronger faith in God than before. It was the daily impulses, prayers and spiritual songs that deepened my relationship with God, just like those numerous prayers and talks during the pilgrimages. From that point on I could no longer deny my desire: I wanted to become a female priest - in the Roman Catholic Church.

In my youthful naivety I thought that after graduating from high school I would study theology, write a few letters to Rome, talk to my professors, and then there would be no more obstacles in my way towards realizing my dream.

The truth of course, I learned only later during the course of my studies, is that there would indeed be giant obstacles. I had to come up with a plan B: waiting, hoping, praying and acting.

The vocation becomes stronger

Soon, I knew that it would not be easy for a female to receive a priesthood and that I had to deal with this situation. For me it was, and still is, a gift from God. I accepted it with gratitude. It was not hard for me to make that choice. There were no lengthy deliberations.

On the contrary: it was obvious to me, that there was something inside me that others of my age did not have (or at least they did not admit to it), and that I would invest all my strength to realize this dream.

As I was aware of the fact, that as a female, I could not (yet) become ordained as a priest, I often struggled with this restriction. I talked with the pastor, the pastoral assistant and with my teacher of religious instruction. Together we deliberated if I ought to convert to the Evangelical Lutheran Church. For me that was ruled out. I am Roman Catholic and I knew that I am called to serve in the Roman Catholic Church, because I consider myself rooted in the Roman Catholic Church. By that time I was a Roman Catholic to the core.

The Catholic understanding of the liturgy and the sacraments was important to me. My feeling was, that a conversion would not be the true path for me. In my youth I decided that my path was to the priesthood. For me there was never a doubt that I would accept this call by God and that I would go through with it. I know that it will not always be easy, but with God's help I will succeed.

He has given me this special gift . He will not leave me alone with it. I have made my decision.

The path to my studies of theology at the university

The news, that I would study theology at university did not

come as a big surprise to any of my friends or to the members of my extended family. After all I had become a pious churchgoing person, who wore sweatshirts with the slogan 'I love Jesus Christ'. I wanted to continue to serve God. In my opinion the best way to do this was to take up an Ecclesiastical profession. I planned to work as a pastoral assistant until females would be permitted to be ordained as priests in the Roman Catholic Church. I considered that an important service too, since it was a testimony of faith.

Nobody in my parish objected to my decision to become a Roman Catholic priest, at least not in an obvious way. Perhaps the faithful thought that this was only a temporary phase and that it would soon vanish.

However, when I began my studies of theology, I soon saw that not everybody considered this a good idea. I had to learn to justify myself.

Nevertheless, this initial phase of justification strengthened my belief, because I had to ask myself again and again, if I had really been called or if I had only imagined it. I learned to deal with that and to stand firm for my faith and my dreams.

Initially there were no conflicts with the professors at the university. However, near the end of my time in Freiburg in Germany, I encountered professors who, it appeared, discriminated against me when it came to grading my work. But I ignored that. I learned a lot from my small conservative circle of friends. Thus, I got a completely different perspective of my goal and I came to the conclusion that the Roman

Catholic Church would not make progress as long as one side was excluded from the dialog. People outside the university respected my approach.

Many people I met do not believe in God or do not want to have anything to do with the Roman Catholic Church. But these people regarded my goal as admirable and courageous. Again and again people say, 'Finally! It is about time a young woman stands up for what is right."

Already in my first semesters at the university I knew a difficult path lay ahead of me. But the positive reaction from so many different people told me the time was ripe to fight, as courageously as possible, for the ministerial priesthood for females and to continue to publicly testify my own vocation.

I would not be myself if I did not stand firm for this calling by God. It has made me the person I am today.

If I concealed my vocation, I would not only deny God and His will, but also I would diminish myself as a person.

The Vocation

Called to be a female priest - is that even possible?

I strongly feel that God has called me to become a priest of the Roman Catholic Church. Such a senstaion is not merely a gut feeling and it is not limited to one single moment in time. Rather it is a slow process where again and again you feel that you are being called. Sometimes that can be scary because you do not know if you are up to the task. At first you experience a feeling that tells you to say yes to the priestly service. To bring about a clarification in this 'initial phase', reflection about the life of a priest is extremely important. I prayed a lot and talked with people I trusted in my parish, with friends and my family.

During this time I wrestled with God in prayer. I put the results of this process into words and brought them up in dialog with spiritual companions. Thereby my relationship with God grew stronger and my vocation became more defined.

The first budding of a vocation is above all a matter of feelings of the heart, which, step-by-step, should be thought through and clarified. It is very hard to describe. Everybody who has been called knows how hard it is to put this into words, for words can never express the entire dimension of what is being experienced. The start of a vocation is a very private, intimate moment between God and the one who is being called. Thereby a yearning for the priestly life begins to grow. In conclusion, I can say openly today, honestly and clearly that I am called to become a female priest in the Roman Catholic Church.

Often, I deliberated whether my vocation could find an expression in some other service within the church. But repeatedly God lead me back to my destiny as a priest. A second sign of a true vocation is the strong motivation to serve and the longing to be there for other people.

In addition, there must be a willingness to place yourself at the service of God and to put your own desires behind those of God. For a priest is ordained for the people and never for him - or herself. To be called means to enter into service for others. If somebody wants to become a priest in order to gain high esteem in his or her family or to gain a highly regarded, respected and powerful position, or if somebody becomes a priest because his family urged him against his will to marry, and he wants to escape from this pressure, this is not a legitimate motive.

A third criterion which can be used to estimate your vocation is your aptitude for priestly service. In this context, university studies of theology as well as your personal ability to inspire enthusiasm about faith in others, play an important role. A person who cannot get on well with others, can hardly serve well as a priest, as it will be his or her task to be there for and to take care of others.

Another consideration for a vocation is its confirmation by other people. It is possible to imagine that you have been called because others convince you it is so. Therefore, an assessment of its authenticity by others is required.

In my case, different people in all situations have confirmed that in their opinion I have been called to serve as a priest in the Roman Catholic Church.

I know I have been called to something that is not

possible so far. But that motivates me to stand up for it. I feel the longing to administer the sacraments and to stand at the altar as a Roman Catholic female priest. If you feel a priestly vocation, you don't feel called primarily to manage a parish, but first to serve within the church - to administer the sacraments and to strengthen the faith of people. Through conversation and prayer one must find out, if the vocation is related to the priestly service or to another service within the church.

I am not the only female who feels called to become a priest in the Roman Catholic Church. Therefore, I struggle neither alone nor in vain. I know that God has given me the task to stand up for a renewal of the Roman Catholic Church. I am not special. After all I am merely one of seven billion people here on our planet. But my dream may seem special.

As an adolescent I thought that I was 'only' enthusiastic about Jesus Christ. But by and by, I noticed that something more was involved. It was a burning for the priestly service.

I had not only the desire to preach, to celebrate the Eucharist, to baptize children, to take confession, to establish marriage and to donate the anointing of the sick, but I felt the call to do so.

Is it presumptive to think something like that and to speak of it? I do not think so. God has given me something great. Even though, under the present circumstances, I cannot completely fulfill my vocation, at least I have the opportunity to do everything to make it real. As an adolescent I thought

I could not be called to a priestly service like a man. After many conversations with priests but also with friends and acquaintances, and after several pilgrimages, I know that a woman can be called to follow God's path. For why should God's call only go out to a man, as God created man and woman and put them on the same level?[1] Did God really make a distinction between these two? Does God not look into the hearts of people?

Called to do what?

When one of my friends asked a priest, if females could be called to the priesthood in the Roman Catholic Church, he answered, "No, that is completely ruled out. Only males can be called to the priesthood by God. Females most certainly not." Those are clear words. But don't they express an enormous presumption? How can he know that God cannot and will not call females to the priesthood?

When females feel called to the priesthood, they should not deny God's call. There is no need for females to hide. God has given us a voice for speaking out. And we should speak clearly and courageously as Jesus Christ did. We know that the call comes from God, not from other people.

It is wrong to say that the vocation of a male is valid and that the vocation of a female is not valid. The Holy Scripture says it clearly, "There is no Jew or Greek, servant or free, male or female: because you are all one in Jesus Christ." (Galatians

3:28).

To be sure, I know that I will not be ordained as a priest of the Roman Catholic Church tomorrow (depending of course when you might be reading this book!). Until that happens I will have to look for another career option. But sometime in the future my vocation will prevail and I will be a priest of the Roman Catholic Church. Of that I am completely certain.

I feel that I have been chosen to stand up for a merciful church, a church that is listened to and that is maintained by young people.

I feel chosen, together with many other faithful in the church, to finally achieve equality of males and females and to open the doors of the priesthood for females.

I may be an inconvenience because I cannot overlook the current defects within the Roman Catholic Church.

In our latitudes being defiant like that does not put your life in danger. But it can get you into unpleasant situations. In the past, or in other parts of the world even today you would be, or are exposed to dangers by showing defiance like this. Thus I believe that it is even more important to show courage here and now. For this is the only way for things to change.

Why not keep silent?

Of course, one might say that I am deluding myself and that I am refusing to let go of an illusion. But I feel something inside me, that is difficult to explain, which actually transcends the dimension of mere written words on a sheet of paper. People may question my vocation and my engagement.

However, I do not consider my vocation a mere fancy. Since I regard my vocation as coming from God - which I cannot prove - I firmly believe that I have been given the courage and endurance necessary to stand up for it.

I regard my vocation as something special. It gives me the strength to raise my voice time and again to fight for my dream. I know that it would be more comfortable for me to be silent and to look for an alternative path. My vision of a church with female priests scandalizes certain conservative circles. However, as I consider the call by God a gift, I act on it with respect and with care, and I do not keep silent. It is time to break the silence and to stand up for a renewed church.

How can a discrimination against females[2] be any longer legitimized in the name of Jesus Christ?

I do not keep silent, for I love the church, and my faith in God is more important to me than an explicit ban on discussion[3].

Chapter Two

The Struggle

Fighting for my dream

Often it appears to me as if insurmountable obstacles are piling up to keep me from realizing my dream. It takes a lot of courage and faith to keep me from turning around or, at least, stopping in front of those obstacles until I come up with a plan to overcome them.

At such times my second passion comes to my assistance: boxing.

In boxing, I have learned not to shy away from the opponent, but to look him in the eye and to fight.

In boxing, I practice to be well prepared for the duel. For me, boxing does not mean I face my opponent with brute force, although clearly boxing is a combat sport and thus force and physical skill are applied. When I am training, it is not my goal to deliberately hurt my opponent but to meet him on an equal footing. Boxing is subject to definite rules, where fairness is essential. You train together with others, you support each other and you help each other to reach a higher level.

If you have a bad day and become aggressive, you may not climb into the ring with a partner. Rather, you must use the punch bag, for otherwise you might hurt your partner.

In the ring, a high degree of concentration is required, as well as respect for the other person. You should keep in mind that, for a fight, you only climb into the ring with a person of the same weight class, the same age and the same combat experience.

In training, you can have more experienced partners in order to learn from them. Sometimes those are also of a higher weight class or of a higher age or of the opposite sex.

Training several times a week is necessary to achieve good results in the boxing ring. Similarly, good university studies of theology are nuts and bolts for effecting changes in the Roman Catholic Church.

This is the way I fight for my vocation.

To stand firm for my vocation in public sometimes means a struggle. Take for instance the parish, where I have lived for some time. The priest knew of my vocation, and he had known me already for some time. A few months before I moved to this parish, I had visited him and offered my help as a lector and as a Communion helper. When after my move to this parish I wrote to him to tell him that I had arrived and that I would like to serve in the church, he ignored me at first, then he thanked me politely for my interest, but told me, that I would have to wait for one year until the new schedules for lectors and

Communion helpers would be set up. He did not even register me as a substitute. I tried, without success, to convince him not to have me wait for one year.

After one year of waiting he could no longer keep me from assisting the parish.

Those are exactly the type of small obstacles that can be put in your path. However, those obstacles cannot stop me.

As in the case of boxing, taking a hard hit is just experience from which you learn and continue. I am hardened and I do not fear setbacks in church. However, I never forget to question my actions and to check again and again if I am doing the right thing and if my views are valid.

I do not only fight for my vocation and its realization in the Roman Catholic Church, but I also fight for God outside the church. To give witness to God in an increasingly godless society often resembles a bitter fight, the expected outcome of which - that the faithful are bound to lose - appears to be determined from the very beginning. But I deliberately render myself open to attack by fielding the questions of non-believers and sometimes bearing their mockery. I have often experienced that in the beginning of a conversation my dialog partner would mock my faith, but nobody ever laughed about my vocation as a priest. It is not my intention to force my faith onto other people.

For me it is sufficient to motivate them to contemplate faith, for if I succeed in this, I have won the 'fight'.

Boxing: lived equality of men and women

Paul and the communities founded by him lived in full equality together. So, he wrote in a letter to the Galatians: "Because you are all sons of God through faith in Christ Jesus, for all those of you, who were given baptism into Christ did put on Christ. There is no Jew nor Greek, servant or free, male or female: because you are all one in Jesus Christ" (Galatians 3:26 pp).

All are saved by Jesus Christ, and all participate in salvation in the same way and to the same extent. Through baptism we are all one in Jesus Christ and we all share in priestly dignity. Given, that someone is, "in Christ (through baptism), then he is in a new world" (II Corinthians 5:17), and therefore is entitled to enter priestly service.

The ability to serve God as a priest is not dependent on sex but is determined by the dignity that God has given to all people. A female can be a representative of the service to Jesus Christ.[4] It may be true that Jesus was male, but first of all he was a human being. We are talking about incarnation, not about 'becoming a male'.

As the emphasis is on incarnation, both males and females can serve to represent Jesus Christ. For we are, "one holy order of priests" (I Peter 2:5) - man and woman together.

It is interesting that the quoted biblical passage from the letter to the Galations is better realized in my boxing club than in the Roman Catholic Church. In boxing, everybody is treated as equal - somebody, who is new in a country and does not speak the national language all that well, just as much as a girl who has only recently joined the boxing club are treated on an equal footing with the regular members of the club. Females have to do as many push-ups as males, and in sparring, females go as many rounds as males. This equality makes us one big team, a family. No matter if German or Serb, Christian or Muslim, woman or man - all are equal.

Fighting for equality

I believe that women in certain areas do not perform as well as men *and men in some areas do not perform as well as women.* I noticed that when my coach told our boxing group after training that every one of us had to do at least ten pull-ups. Since I am quite incapable of doing pull-ups, I kept silent to avoid having to do this exercise. The other three women, who were participating in the training that day followed my example. A fourteen-year-old boxing companion noticed that and he said: "And the girls? They must do pull-ups as well. You always want equality. Here you have got it."

His words were clear. It became clear to me, that there are things, that are more difficult to do for women. Although on the other hand there are also things in sports that women can do better than men, for instance tasks related to mobility. However, it will probably take me years to learn to perform a decent pull-up. In this area, the hoped-for equality of sexes fails, if one wants to interpret it like that.

But it may be regarded as a first step towards equality that a man offered me the opportunity to do pull-ups rather than exclude me from this exercise just because I am a woman.

I can imagine that the opponents of female priesthood in the Roman Catholic Church will jump up and use these words against me: "You see, females cannot do everything, they are not 'able' to do everything. Therefore, it is not possible for females to be ordained as priests in the Roman Catholic Church." However, those are two different pairs of shoes. I stand up for giving women as well as men in all cultures and all areas of life the opportunity to develop their abilities and to use their talents.

If physical obstacles exist, then it is up to the woman *or the man* themselves to decide, what to do about it. After all it is up to them to make a career and/or to stay home to raise their children.

That night I did not exercise on the bar. And I kept my silence and watched the men doing pull-ups. The men in the boxing club offered me equal opportunities, which I rejected because I knew at that moment that they represented a major obstacle to me. Regarding my dream to become a priest in the Roman Catholic Church, the only obstacle is the teaching of the Roman Catholic Church and the regulation rooted in the ecclesiastical law (Codex iuris Canonici from 1983) that only baptized males are entitled to receive the ordination to the priesthood (Canon 1024). This obstacle will have to be surmounted sooner or later as the authorities of the Roman Catholic Church can no longer hide behind arguments which are theologically, legally and socially unsustainable.

I believe that there are three levels of equality for women:

The first level states that equal rights for women imply opportunities that may be regarded as a matter of course, like driving a car or performing pull-ups. In both cases the women are offered the opportunity to do something.

The second level of equality is the perception of having equal rights. If a woman does not want to drive a car, that is okay. Potentially she is allowed to do it and is able to do it, if she has learned it, as every man has to learn it, *too*. Both levels go together. It is important that women as well as men have the chance to decide for themselves.

The third level is the legal permission to do something. In the case of driving a car, permission is granted by the law of the state.

In the case of the Roman Catholic Church, the Codex Iuris Canonici as a kind of ecclesiastical law does not allow women to be ordained to the priesthood. The third level of equality is therefore not realized in the Roman Catholic Church.

Today's females have already achieved a great variety of possibilities through gender equality. The Charter of Human Rights is, thank God, untouchable by the Roman Catholic Church.

Imagine the way things were about 100 years ago: at that

time women fought for the basic right to self-determination. They stood up for political participation. And today together with many other women[5].I stand up for equality, equal rights and gender equality in the Roman Catholic Church.

I will not use violent or hate speech to realize my vocation, but love, humility and humbleness.

I think it is time for women to stand up and have their say. Always keeping in mind that Jesus Christ, in whose succession we call ourselves Christians, did not announce the coming of the Kingdom of God with hate, but with love and humility.[6]

Through fighting we can effect changes: with patience and in the hope of the acting of the Holy Spirit even in a time like today.

A pointless struggle?

A boxing companion once told me: "Your entire campaign is just a drop in the ocean. It is no use if you stand up and say that you want to become a female priest. As if the Roman Catholic Church is going to change because of that. Chances are that you are just going to mortgage your future and waste your energy that way." I see it differently: If everybody had always kept silent when they were confronted with apparently impossible tasks, we would not stand where we are today.

Presumably women would still not be permitted to vote

in Europe and the ecclesiastical law would still demand that women should cover their heads in order to be allowed to enter a church.[7]

I believe it is important that every individual stands up for something. Even if at first it seems to be no use, it may perhaps take effect in the future. Anybody can place a stone and eventually many stones will form a strong and firm foundation that becomes a huge building. However, a foundation is stable and able to hold a load, only if it has been set up correctly; the individual parts should be firmly connected. Thus, not only patience and effort are needed but also an architect who designs, accompanies and monitors the construction. In addition, sufficient know-how and precisely calculated statics are required. A good foundation needs many things, but here as everywhere else the saying "nothing ventured, nothing gained" holds true. This is the only way that progress is possible.

When I was in Poland and was attending a seminar together with many priests and female students of theology, my euphoria to become a female priest decreased considerably and reality caught up with me fast. Is all my effort perhaps a pointless struggle doomed to fail?

I had to realize, that the priesthood of females is just not on the agenda in Poland, at least not at the moment. After I have been thrown in at the deep end and had to realize that in Poland perhaps it was not time yet for female priests at the altar, it crossed my mind that nothing is impossible for

God (Matth 19:26). Presently, the Roman Catholic Church in Poland still has many members, and faith is still being lived.

But even Roman Catholic Poland shows a tendency of a decrease of the number of churchgoers. In recent years more and more adolescents can no longer relate to the church, because the church no longer appeals to them.

I have enjoyed my brief stay in Poland because I felt incredibly happy surrounded by all those priests, those faithful and with those full churches. Even though my vocation and my wish to be ordained as a female priest encountered a lack of understanding, I was received in a friendly manner. Not everybody showed a negative attitude when I stated my vocation. I believe that sooner or later, even in Poland, people are going to think differently about female priesthood.

Would a female have dared to utter such a wish 150 years ago in Germany? Hardly.

The Pope: a provoker

Pope Francis has made an announcement with the choice of his name. Since the beginning of his pontificacy the comfortable attitude of the pope as a lord and the associated secure nest of power and wealth are both history. He fights with a brave heart and with a clear end in view. Therefore, for many people Francis' demeanor appears as a provoker. Some people regard me too as a provoker. Why do I presume as a young woman to stand up for female priesthood, when I could easily enter a convent?

People who provoke will always be inconvenient to those who try to avoid any change. Francis stands up for a renewed self-image of the Roman Catholic Church. Through this provocation he irritates many people and makes them reconsider their opinions. With charm and a smile he shakes seemingly unsurmountable walls. For him it is clear that a provocation can never be gentle or else it would lose its impact.

I want to provoke on behalf of equality brought to the people by Jesus Christ and on behalf of gender equality that already existed in the early church.[8]

Revolutionary struggle

Many people want a revolution, in particular in the church. People are eagerly looking to Rome. With high hopes, they expect groundbreaking renewals. I too am looking towards Rome. And I very much hope, that the discussions about the position and the dignity of females within the church will once more be on the agenda. In this I expect that not only motherhood and virginity are considered[9], but finally, also the entire female existence. It is time to listen to women and to take them seriously in their vocation.

It will require a fight to push through such a revolution, which in turn requires your own participation. Most people would agree with a change, but very few of them will join the revolutionary fight. However, only if you stand up for your heart's desire, it will someday become real.

Boxing is my hobby. Therefore, fighting in the church comes easy to me. I don't do that out of frustration or hate, but out of passion and love.

I Can Wait
Waiting but acting

For me preserving traditions is important. I do not want tradition to be no more than a small heap of cold ashes, but a fire that gives people guidance and that touches the heart. In order for tradition to stay awake and alive, it has to be changeable. It must always be considered and realized according to the "signs of the times" (Gaudium et Spes, No. 4). Tradition must never be allowed to 'freeze', otherwise it would be like an exhibit in an antiquarian bookshop or in a museum. Thomas More (1478-1535) said: "Tradition is not to preserve the ashes but to pass on the flame."

At the same time, a currently lived tradition must be scrutinized. From history we learn, why and how things have developed into what they are today. For example, to understand the acts of Jesus it is necessary to know about the time before He appeared.

And therefore, the topic of 'women and the church' is not merely a problem of the women who have been called to the priesthood, but most of all a problem of the church itself, as it undermines the credibility of the Roman Catholic Church.

In theory equality is being preached (see Galatians 3:28; Lumen Gentium No. 32; Gaudium et Spes No. 29: "Nevertheless, with respect to the fundamental rights of the person, every type of discrimination, whether social or cultural, whether based on sex, race, color, social condition, language or religion, is to be overcome and eradicated as contrary to God's intent."; Canon 208 CIC 1983: "There exists among all the Christian faithful a true equality") but in practice it is easy to see that there is a long way to go towards its realization. The church is asked to resolve this dilemma by speaking an understable language and providing plausible arguments for its position. And if the position is to not change anything about the tradition, one should justify that to the people. History itself has shown repeatedly how changeable tradition can be.

An event that ushered in large-scale change was the second Vatican Council.[10] It did not break with tradition but it interpreted it in a new way to ensure that it still has effective force and that its fire is not lost.

History of the Roman Catholic Church shows us, that things have not always been as they are today. Procedures taken from days past can be relevant and helpful for the progress of the church today, without disregarding new 'phenomena'. The respective environment has always influenced the church and changed its structure. To adapt is one way to deal with challenges. Another more fundamental way is faith.

Faith is "A light to be recovered"[11], as it has been written in the encyclical letter Lumen Fidei by Pope Francis. Maybe it is time to have the courage to allow us to be guided by that light. To not force anything but just trust and believe. However, that does not mean that one ought to sit back and take things easy and refuse to act. The reflection on the life of Jesus Christ is always important in this regard. His way of dealing with people and His dedication to the people and to God's manifest greatness. When we look back to Jesus Christ, to the origins of our faith, it becomes easier for us to look ahead.

The church is allowed to stay true to its tradition and it should never forget that, because failing to regard tradition will lead to a loss of focus on the consensus of our faith.

Progress does not necessarily imply a break with what was before. Rather progress means to be true to our 2000-year-old tradition. That progress occured in the liturgical and theological renewal of the last century. Reform served to enrich the tradition of the church, thus bringing about positive change. This progress also showed that there were people in the church who, based on tradition, were ready to use their critical minds to approach new challenges. Without a renewal, there will be no permanent passing-on of the faith.

Tradition is important, but we must not cling to it. Rather, we must let ourselves be guided by it.

If tradition was merely rigid, there would never have been any changes within the church. History will always bring forth something new, and thus the history of Christianity through the centuries has caused changes time and again. The first Christians were circumcised as they were mostly Jewish Christians. Following the apostle Paul, circumcision was no longer mandatory as an unconditional characteristic of the faithful Christians. Paul already brought a different tradition from Damascus and Antioch to early Christianity that came into conflict with that of Peter in Jerusalem. In the New Testament different traditions can be found side by side, which the first editors of the Holy Scripture already could not unify without breaks. Thus, the question arose, which of those traditions should be considered as valid.

Before the second Vatican Council, the Community at the table as it is described in the Holy Scripture was performed with the priest celebrating with his back to the congregation. After the second Vatican Council, it became customary to celebrate mass in the local language, and the priest now celebrates Eucharist facing the congregation. In the history of the church there have always been several traditions (tradition of dogma, tradition of folk belief, spiritual-mystical tradition, tradition of ritual, liberal tradition) side by side, which in part were and still are in conflict with each other.

Where it serves one's own agenda and options, one often helps oneself from all those strands of traditions by picking and choosing individual elements while skipping and passing over others. However, it was not only liturgical discourses and their theological meaning that changed, but also the architecture of churches. Ecclesiastical art kept up with the times and with the needs of the people. The unpretentious Romanesque churches were succeeded by Gothic towers standing strident against the sky. In the baroque period the interior of churches was designed with splendor, gold and color. In the year 1983 a new canon law was introduced, in which some canons from the former canon law of 1917 were removed, for instance the part stating that the confession of a female could only be taken in a church, but never in private rooms.[12] The change of direction of the Roman Catholic Church concerning religious freedom following the second Vatican council was much more dramatic. With the granting of religious freedom in the declaration Dignitatis Humanae (1965) the dictum of a 'duty towards the true' was superseded. Until the second Vatican council, a heresy was dogmatically condemned. After that the 'right of person' was strengthened and the individual freedom of conscience, the right and the duty to seek and accept the truth, superseded the compulsion legitimized under the label of 'truth'. Thus, religious freedom became a basic value of the church doctrine. Clearly tradition is never something rigid and static.

Tradition motivates us to act innovatively and to forge new paths.

One could list many such changes of tradition that occurred in 2000 years of history of the Roman Catholic Church. These changes sometimes need a lot of time and adequate preparation. To make a change successful requires the courage to accept the new and to take hitherto unknown paths.

Today the time is ripe for female priests and for married priests in the Roman Catholic Church. That means that authorities in the Roman Catholic Church need to look for and adopt new ways to achieve those goals.

Waiting needs patience

Once a fellow student inquired somewhat tauntingly and derogatively: "What do you think are the chances that the Roman Catholic Church will ever ordain women as priests?" I merely replied: "My hope is as big as a grain of mustard seed." A grain of mustard seed is tiny. For the tiny grain of seed to grow into a big fertile plant both time and resilience are required. The seed must be sown at the right time. If the ground is too dry, it will not sprout. It has to be planted in good, fertile earth, and it needs a lot of care for this grain of seed to grow into a magnificent plant. If all those requirements are met, the tiny grain of seed may become the strong, healthy plant that produces an abundance of mustard seeds.

Sometimes, to be honest, I consider my wish to become an ordained female priest in the Roman Catholic Church as something impossible. Let us bear in mind that the first female pastoral assistants were introduced only 40 years ago, and that it has been a stony path and a hard struggle for women to get there. We owe the profession of a pastoral assistant to the second Vatican Council, which newly emphasized the responsibility and the participation of lay persons in the church.[13] The commitment of women and men for this profession and its acceptance has proven worthwhile. Patience has never been one of my dominant virtues. However, concerning the realization of my vocation, I believe that I have got the patience, the resilience and the necessary endurance required. I am patient with the Roman Catholic Church and I have faith in the Holy Spirit, that He will make things happen when the time is right. Until then I prepare myself for everything and I will be prepared. After all, in The Epistle of Paul the Apostle to the Hebrews it is stated: "For, having done what was right in God's eyes, you have need of waiting before his word has effect for you" (Hebrews 10:36).

Chapter Three

Renewal and Change in the Church

Reform of the heart

A true, real and effective reform always starts inside, in the heart. I long for reformers of the heart, who will advance the church and make it flourish in the 21st century. This depends on the postive actions of everybody, not least on young people, to do what is right. It is my firm conviction that it is worthwhile to stand up for the faith. Without that conviction, would I have so much power and endurance?

I cannot standby and permit the church to completely lose its value, and I cannot permit faith in Jesus Christ to become a taboo subject in our societies. I stand up and fight for a lively, young church, a church liked by young and old together. I advocate a church to which people will listen again and which will play an important role in the lives of people. I want to be a reformer of the heart.

A new color for the church

During mass, a priest preached about the advertising slogan of a brand of skates. He applied the buzzwords *color, deepness* and *contrast* to the church and found, that these features are exactly what the church needs. Our church needs color, deepness and contrast. As Christians we have to show our true colors, for without color we cannot shine. In many ways the church needs a new coat of paint and new dimensions, and it has to contrast with its surroundings. These three components - color, deepness and contrast - are features of a successful product. However, the church needs to examine time and again if there are not any additional dimensions to take into account.

Everybody can participate in the development of the church. In many parishes there are successful examples of how to realize that. When I think of my home parish the large number of altar servers comes to mind. We had our own band of altar servers who regularly performed in a well-attended youth mass. By introducing new spiritual songs that everybody could sing along with, and through the participation of altar servers and young people, who helped to organize the youth masses, going to mass became more appealing. This is just one example how one can replenish church rooms. In many parishes creativity is emphasized. I believe that this creativity that serves to revive the church should be given greater prominence.

Church life must become more attractive. The church

should not deter people. Rather people should be comfortable in the church. To me that means that the church needs to gain a new appeal, so that people can feel at home in the church. Is it not pleasant to collaborate in building a house, knowing that your work, your power and your sweat will contribute? The courage for creating the future appearance of the church cannot be allowed to continue to lose impetus. The quality of the future church depends on young people who will shape the church in such a way, that they can feel at home in it. And by inspiring the church with an entirely new spirit, no longer will God be imprisoned in the church, but He will be carried into the whole world. Of course, I understand the frustration of people who say that they have tried and that after meeting a strong resistance time and again, they do not want to invest further effort into the development of the church.

Often in fields such as economics and politics, both in the church and in the world, the male influence is too many times given primacy.

The Roman Catholic Church could exert a positive influence on society if it stood up for equal opportunity for everybody. Christianity could form an idea of the human being, that would have influence far beyond the church. As the Roman Catholic Church declares a message of liberation and equality, it must lead the way towards lived gender equality. However, at the moment the church lags behind society considerably. I believe that female priests will add new color to the church and be part of its greater revival. Different facets will make our church colorful and appealing to many people. Different depths will give the church new images and perspectives. The Church has so many dimensions which we must enhance.

The community of the faithful consists of individuals. That makes it so unique. Everybody has the same right and also the task to collaborate in the building of God's kingdom. Everybody can contribute in the development of the church. Everything depends on the faithful. This way, the church will be brought alive, and it will become future-oriented, variegated and colorful.

Reform of thinking

It is my opinion - especially as this concerns me personally - that the church needs holistic thinking. This can only be achieved when men and women are allowed to contribute equally. The Roman Catholic Church cannot be allowed to continue with its gender-discriminatory system of offices. Patriarchal structures need to be broken up. The church has a long way to go until real reforms will be achieved. If some day married priests are ordained in the Roman Catholic Church, in some parishes it will require a bit of time until they are accepted and respected as fully adequate priests. How long will it then take for women to be accepted as fully adequate (married) priests?

Through my activities as a speaker, I get direct insight into the lives of different congregations. There I meet not only kindred spirits, but also critics of the idea of a reform of the Roman Catholic Church.

Thus an older man told me with regard to the topic of celibacy, that he would never accept the Holy Communion given by a married priest. The reason he gave for this refusal was that a married priest could pollute the altar bread, if he had been together with his wife the night before.

This statement made me realize how some people still embrace a way of thinking that is deeply rooted in categories like 'pure' and 'impure'.

Although the abuse scandals of the last years have badly shaken the image of the 'pure priest' and priests have been stripped of their enchantment as 'saints', in certain circles a way of thinking still dominates that concedes a male 'more' purity than a female. Women are branded as unclean due to their menstruation. As long as such a way of thinking is not broken up, it will be difficult to establish married priests (male and female) in parishes. In order to change this way of thinking, a continuous process of enlightenment will be required. Only when the way of thinking has changed, reforms will be accepted. Before everything else a reform of thinking is required!

Church Today - Church Tomorrow

"Go and repair my house"

When as an adolescent I visited Assisi together with my parish and stood in front of the small church S. Damiano looking at the crucifix, about which it is told, that the savior asked Holy Francis of Assisi to "go and repair My house", I was deeply moved.

During this journey those words came back to me time and again, and I asked myself: Can I also contribute to the rebuilding of the Church? At first Francis of Assisi thought, that he was supposed to literally reconstruct the church building, which lay in ruins. So he began to erect the broken down walls again. But that was not what the call had meant. Francis was meant to change the spirit of the church and to contribute to the renewal of the church. This call implied the end of a self-centered church. With his lifestyle Francis of Assisi challenged the centralized and clericalized Roman Catholic system. This would be the beginning of a true succession of Jesus Christ in poverty and humility. The return to the cause of Jesus Christ was central. He saw the faults all too clearly and felt that he was called to criticize them. He wanted to raise again a church that was indulging in wealth and grandeur, and he emphasized the Christian roots in it. However, in this he was not really successful. Rome pruned and incorporated him and his order. The holy Francis withdrew in bitterness and even distanced himself from his order.

But I refuse to be discouraged by such setbacks of the past. I have devoted myself to the construction of the church. I consider it my task to find ways and chances to build a church, which offers equal opportunities to women and men, and where young people can find a home. I contribute to build a church, which overcomes discrimination in its own ranks, and a church, that enables me to live my vocation.

Francis of Assisi was written off as a nut-case by some villagers, when he gave away his worldly possessions and turned his back on his rich father. He succeeded in living his vision of the church. During my week in Assisi I experienced the will to renew the church. Time and again I asked God in prayer: "What is it that I can do? How am I supposed to rebuild Your church?" Francis of Assisi is of assistance to me in answering this question: He listened to his heart and he acted.

Sweating to build a new church

Renewal means work and labor, sweat and effort. In order to renew or to improve something, one has to stick together rather than walk around in egotistic delusions. Everybody within the church, however unimportant, contributes to build the church. In the future, each individual will be able to contribute, too. But is this effort worthwhile? Should I waste all my energy on the church, which, at least in Western Europe, has little or no future?

As the church is like a family to me, any effort for it is worthwhile. You stand up with great effort for the people you love. I do not want the church to lose its importance, nor do I want faith to lose its radiance. I will have to "sweat" a lot, until I can fulfil my dream. However, then I will know that it has been worthwhile.

The shaping of the earth and of the church is the task put upon us by God, a task that will never be easy, but it will be practicable. For it is God, who always speaks the first and the last word.

I firmly believe, that my labors will not be in vain.

Giving testimony for Jesus Christ out of solidarity with persecuted Christians

Today persecution of Christians continues but is certain places it is worse than ever. According to estimates about one hundred million Christians are being persecuted in more than fifty countries.[14] In Europe and in the United States we do not need to be afraid of persecution; we do not even have to testify to our faith. However, exactly for that reason I consider it all the more important for us to learn again to give voice to our faith and to our religion. In other countries of the world people die because they are Christians. We send out a signal of solidarity when we not only think of and pray for these people, but also publicly declare ourselves to be their brothers and sisters. Certainly, this is going to remain a purely verbal action for the most part. But I think that will be a first step. For we are brothers and sisters because we are humans and have faith in Jesus Christ.

Talking about faith

In a time when there are almost daily reports about religiously motivated terrorism to be found in the media, we as Christians must raise our voices more clearly than ever. How often did I have to read in the newspapers during recent months that Christians had been murdered because of their faith; at the same time, as dedicated Christians we recognize the suffering of those of other faiths such Muslims killed in Syria, Iraq and other countries of the world, they should not be forgotten. The peaceful followers of every faith in God must be supported and we do that best by having the courage to talk about our faith and about the religion to which we belong.

I am proud to be a Christian and I like to be Roman Catholic. I will let everybody know that. I wear my crucifix on a necklace, thus bearing witness to my faith through a gem. But I also put it in words. I have the courage to tell everybody that I am a faithful Christian, and I stand up for it, no matter what other people think of me.

We live in a society that affords us the privilege to openly speak about our faith. Many Christians of the world do not enjoy that privilege. Nevertheless, they stand firm in their faith in Jesus Christ. In some states they meet secretly to celebrate mass, and in doing so they risk their safety if not their lives. Since many Christians are not allowed to publicly bear witness, we have to emphasize that we belong to them. It is to be hoped that this approach will be effective and helpful.

The Joy of Faith
My life with Jesus Christ

Ever since as an adolescent I moved to and joined a new parish I consider Jesus Christ a friend, who accompanies me in my life. My faith gives me strength and joy. I could never imagine not to believe. I am a person who always had a lot of energy. And thus I was asked many times, why I am always in such a good mood and how is it I can talk and act in an inspirational way. The reason, why I am like this, is: Jesus Christ.

People who do understand little about faith, look at me sort of baffled. I then explain that it is my faith in God that gives me that tireless energy. My faith in Jesus Christ and in his good news gives me strength and joy. At the end of mass I am radiant with joy for I carry Christ within me. The eucharist gives me strength - the strength to follow a path which I know will not be an easy one.

Since Christ came into my life, faith in God is connected to my identity. If I did not believe any more and did not feel this, what would I do? I studied theology with the goal to serve God and His church. I stand up for the ordination of females as priests because I want to serve as a priest, and I pray to God, because He is the one, who makes all that possible. Jesus Christ is the center of my life. And it is His love, that makes me profess the joy of faith.[15] I take my joy from the love of God. I never tire of worshiping God, for I take my strength from prayer and from faith. My life with God is like the air to breathe. Without Him I "would not be able to breathe spiritually"[16]. The eucharist gives me a lot of energy, for me it is the spring of life.[17]

The thirst for God

I believe that, more than ever, people are looking for spirituality and religiosity. This can be seen from the great supply of esoterism. Today an individual patchwork-religion appears to be en-vogue, where a concrete religious denomination or creed are considered a burden rather than a chance for developing one's own concept of living. But even there exists a desire that wants to be fulfilled. I notice that many young people are looking for the meaning of life, for faith, stability and self-confidence. They are looking for something to quench their thirst. However, they do not believe, that faith in the triune God can quench their thirst. For many young people consider it 'uncool' to believe in God. Recently I have experienced an example of such an assessment of faith as 'uncool'. Before a boxing contest of two sporting companions I walked over to them to wish them courage. During that conversation, I told them that they could pray to gain inner strength. One of them, a 14-year-old boy, immediately retorted: "Oh, pray to God? Come on, get serious, that is totally uncool, I don't need any God, I will win anyway." The other one, a 14-year-old girl, looked at me wide-eyed, but did not comment, presumably because she did not want to be regarded as 'uncool'.

The group dynamics of adolescents often decides, whether the desire for faith can be fulfilled or not. I believe that the Christian faith can quench the thirst of those people looking for the meaning of life. I myself have experienced in my youth, how much strength I gained from my faith. That has not changed to this today. I quench my thirst by living my faith and by talking about it openly. I believe that the desire for meaning and faith can only be quenched when a conversation, an exchange with others of faith and also with God takes place.

The joy of Sundays

I do not know how often I left church after service and looking deliberately at the faces of people could not detect an ounce of joy. Friedrich Nietzsche (1844-1900) said: "Christians ought to look much more saved"[18]. Unfortunately, he is right. To be honest I must admit, that I myself have often left the church with a grumpy expression on my face, since for me the mass had not been a joyful celebration, but rather an hour of sorrow and suffering. When I visited the church of my sister's parish on Christmas, I departed filled with indignation. On such a high feast day, the priest had not been able to proclaim God's glorious message. The mass, featuring only songs that were hardly known, took less than 45 minutes and resembled a tragedy. How can the faith in Jesus Christ be passed on joyfully, if joy is lacking in the hearts of the faithful? Christendom awards us exactly that joy to pass it on generously.

Sunday mass is a feast of joy. Near the entrance of a church, there are usually large public squares, where young people sit. If as an outsider, I watched a group of people leaving the church with bowed heads and grumpy faces, it would be understandable, that I would not want to belong to such a congregation. To show the outside world or those who linger around the church building what joy a Sunday mass brings, we must be able to leave the church filled with joy. After all, in this hour together with God we are told about the joyful message. Is that not a sufficient cause to be joyous?

Pope Francis writes: "There are Christians whose lives seem like Lent without Easter."[19] As we are baptized and have heard from Jesus Christ, we should not, and are not allowed to be grumpy. Rather we should joyfully testify our faith.

When Christians are filled with joy and filled with vim and vigor for their faith and for the church, others can get caught up in it. As pope Francis, in his first apostolic exhortation says, the joy of the Gospel must be carried into all the world. How could one do that better than with a smiling face and a burning heart?

Fortunately, not everywhere in the church a depressive

mood is predominant. There is also lived joy: World Youth Day is a great symbol for that. There you find many young people who praise God, together in prayer and in silence, who sing songs and dance on the tables. Faith is not only quiet, although silence is important, too. In Christian events, lived joy is experienced. Back in the day-to-day life of the parish it is often difficult to pass on this joy.

"To celebrate God"

The joy given to us by Jesus Christ is a good starting point to encourage young people to embrace faith.

Certainly, since young people want to enjoy life and since Christians want to celebrate it through the resurrection, there is some intersection. Is not joy of the faith a bit like "partying"? Through the resurrection we have cause, we are even invited, to be joyous and to celebrate. During mass, we celebrate, that God has become one of us and that he has overcome death. Youth masses are a well-accepted current model to make church attendance more modern and peppier. What could be the objection to having a party after mass? Just consider the gospel services; for example, in Harlem or in Africa the party already takes place while the service is in progress. Young people usually need a reason to celebrate and they need somebody with whom they can 'celebrate'. Why not Jesus? Often I have been in a disco and I told myself: I celebrate Jesus. I celebrate Him, because He gives me so much joy in life. Once I went there together with a few friends. A young man noticed my Crucifix necklace, that I always wear, and he asked me if I believe in God. He considered it impressive that Christians can celebrate, too. The idea that Christians are not joyous people, must be overcome. Celebrating offers space to profess your faith. Christians are allowed to party, because God has demonstrated, that death is not the end.

I believe that we need a new understanding of celebrating for young people. Perhaps young people have a different understanding of celebration than older people. A new way of 'celebrating God', by offering the chance to visit the disco together after mass certainly is not an overwhelming recipe for success, but this would perhaps be a good starting point to render the church more attractive for the coming generation. "It is the fate of Christians to sow a lot and to harvest little" (cf. Matthew 13:1-9). However, at least we have to start sowing again, for otherwise we will soon have no harvest at all.

Discovery of God

Many parishes are dominated by a certain severity that presents a challenge for young parents and their children. In the past, for children the exploration of God took place in silence. You accompanied your parents to mass, quietly sat in the pew and paid attention more or less diligently during the service. Today, on the other hand, most children do not want to remain seated. Rather, they want to move around, they want to take a good look at everything, sometimes they even want to giggle or shout. I think that children ought to be allowed to walk around in the church. They ought to be permitted to explore everything and thus to look for and to find God. My friend called this "discovery of God". She herself found faith in this manner. She grew up in a parish in Belgium, where it was considered quite normal for children to run through the church, to enter the altar area and to sit down next to the priest. This attitude of the priest and of the parish towards the children offered the possibility for my friend to remain connected to the church and to find her own faith. She always liked to go to mass, because she knew that she could move freely there and could converse with the priest during the sermon, when she had questions. This is one way of finding God and developing a sense of belonging to the church. Unless we want to risk to lose the younger generation altogether, we will have to tolerate a crying child sitting behind us during mass. Is it not nice when parents attend mass together with their children and thus make the quiet service come alive? Children need to be given space to find their faith. After all Jesus Christ said: "Let the little children come to me" (Luke 18:16).

The Path

A path towards tolerance

I have fellow students, who are ultra conservative or even reactionary. They tell me openly and honestly, that they would leave the Roman Catholic Church if I were to be allowed to be ordained a priest. This was not meant as a personal affront against me. No, it is just that they cannot imagine to see women at the altar of the Roman Catholic Church. For them it is as strange as for others to see a woman wearing a burka. I feel that tolerance is required, not least from students of theology. I regard tolerance as a foundation of our society, a society which is pluralistic and which becomes ever more diverse. How are we to start a dialog with other cultures, religions or opinions, if we lack tolerance and openness in trivialities?

A candidate for the priestly ministry of a German diocese told me, that he would immediately become a member of the Pius-Brotherhood, if the Roman Catholic Church were to ordain females as priests. He let me know unambiguously that this could not be the will of the church. In his opinion it is 'intended by the Roman Catholic Church' that certain groups are being marginalized. According to him, the church would betray its own teachings, if it allowed the ordination of female priests.

Although I do not like this opinion, I am convinced, that to make honest discussion possible you owe your opponents a certain openness towards their ideas. This is the only way to broaden your horizon. We have to concentrate on the positive and on those things we share in common.

The Roman Catholic Church will need a better understanding of tolerance.

Where will the path lead us?

Only if we again induce enthusiasm for faith in young people, the church will stay alive and thrive Young people are the church of tomorrow, in their great and colorful diversity. Young people will pass on the church to their descendants. If the dedicated youth is missing it is easy to realize what the imminent danger to the Roman Catholic Church will be: a further decrease of the number of church-goers since we will all grow old and die. Then what?

The youth in the Western World has been born into an environment that enjoys equal rights. It does not know any fundamental discrimination against women any more. Tomorrow's girls will have the same chances as the boys. How will they be able to feel happy, if they do not encounter this 'innate' equality within the Roman Catholic Church?

In my opinion, the current situation of the church in the Western World can only develop in two possible directions: Either the remaining Christians will turn into a "little flock" (Luke 12:32), or else the church will slowly but surely perish. The situation is a different one when we consider the entire world: the number of Christians in Asia and Africa is increasing steadily[20].

One does not need to be a great prophet to realize, that in the future people will continue to leave the Roman Catholic Church. Nevertheless, I am sure that one can mobilize and fascinate people for the cause of Jesus Christ and the church. In my home parish, I have experienced that myself. After all I have found my faith through the enthusiasm of other faithful. Fewer and fewer young people participate actively in the life of the parishes. However, when an adolescent of today attends mass and stands in front of his peers and openly announces: "Yes, I believe in God, and I attend mass", then he is involved with all his heart. Such people, who find that courage in a society deeply critical of the church, have to be much more supported and strengthened by the church.

If the Roman Catholic Church in the Western World turns into a "little flock", what will that "little flock" look like concretely? Will it consist of 'conservatives', since the 'liberals' will already have left the church? Or will the 'conservatives' actively drive away the dissenters, as they do not see a place for them in the little flock? Certainly a little flock has positive aspects, too. However, it is my opinion, that the church should better remain a big flock, and that the Christians - especially in countries, where Christianity is in decline - should stand up for keeping the Roman Catholic Church alive. In Europe and in the United States the Roman Catholic Church will become attractive again only if and when it manages to reach out to the lives of people through genuine pastoral care, which consists of practical help in everyday life. People do not look to Rome and follow its orders. Rather they expect the clerical authorities to follow their lead.

The path of a journey

To take a journey can mean to take a new path. Sometimes a

path that you have hardly heard about before. In order to stay alive the Roman Catholic Church needs a change. We may accept that as a gift from God, and we do not need to fight against it. We need people who talk and act with credibility. If you keep your eyes open, you will see that there are people who bear witness to the Christian faith in a vivid manner. Only in this vivid way it is possible to build a relationship with God and to share it in a Christian community. However, most importantly: let us be humble, modest, respectful and let us meet the world and the people with love. The journey towards God becomes a journey towards the people. Gospel is a message of joy and of liberation. It is a message for the future. The church incorporates many diverse worlds which are subsumed under one great entity.

Pope Francis offers the people credibility and a new simplicity, that everybody can comprehend and live. This simplicity can be realized without great effort in daily life: it begins in the morning, when you contemplate whether to drive to the baker by car or by bicycle, in order to get your breakfast. For me that question does not arise, as I have no car nor a bicycle, and in a university city you can go far by public transport. When I lived in Germany, I shared a bicycle with others. Small things in life can make a difference. However, that comes to nothing, unless the entire system is challenged, as Jesus Christ already challenged the system of the Pharisees and the scribes.

Pope Francis does this by stating in his Apostolic

Exhortation "Evangelii Gaudium" (2013) that "Such an economy kills" (No.53). When mercy, love and modesty have a place in our daily life, then they will also find a space in the church and in society. However, first and foremost the church must be a role model, to inspire people and show them what it is worth to live in a merciful and humble way.

The path of confrontation

The way the church needs to go, is the path of confrontation. For each reformer, who wants to go a new way, there are others, who are afraid to move far away from home, and who drive to their destination reluctantly with the brakes on. There will always be reactionaries standing in the way of reformers, and there will always be liberals trying to force unconditional progress. On the path of confrontation, it is important to keep in mind, that the church is a church for the people. I wish for a church that does not marginalize anybody. In mutual dialog and in mutual respect the path of confrontation can become a common path, that does not exclude anybody and respects the interests of many.

I am aware of the fact, that not everybody wants to walk on such a common path. There are many, that want to take their own way and turn away from the 'common path' of the church, and who in special cases will even initiate a counter-reaction. Even so I wish for a church, where everybody finds his or her place, today more than ever the question arises, is will this not damage the church? Should the church really include everybody: even neo-fascists who clearly act against the message of Jesus Christ? Do even Nazis, who depreciate other people because of their religion and origin, have their place within the church?

Pope Francis has imposed an anathema, that is to say a ban by the church on the organized crime of the mafia. Members of the mafia are no longer part of the community of the Roman Catholic Church, since their abominable deeds are incompatible with the gospel.

I regard the roof of the church as huge, but its limits are imposed by the message of Jesus Christ.

Jesus also demanded that his fellow humans must change in order to find their place under that roof. If mercy, tolerance, love of the neighbor and love of God are neglected, the roof of the church cannot shape a community. There will always be people who do not want or who are not able to fit under that roof that stands for a unity-in-diversity. However, the church should continue to make comprehensive offers, rather than allow itself to shrink to the size of a thimble, that will cover only the 'favored few'. Watchfulness is needed to prevent right-wing groups from creeping under the roof of the church and labeling themselves as 'Christian'. In the pastoral constitution Gaudium et spes (No.76) it says: "It is very important, especially where a pluralistic society prevails, that there be a correct notion of the relationship between the political community and the Church, and a clear distinction between the tasks which Christians undertake, individually or as a group, on their own responsibility as citizens guided by the dictates of a Christian conscience, and the activities which, in union with their pastors, they carry out in the name of the Church. The Church, by reason of her role and competence, is not identified in any way with the political community nor bound to any political system. She is at once a sign and a safeguard of the transcendent character of the human person. The Church and the political community in their own fields are autonomous and independent from each other." With respect to groups such as the German 'Pegida' which label themselves as 'Christian', but which act against the gospel, Karl Rahner's and Herbert Vorgrimler's comment on the above quote are relevant: "Since the Church cannot forbid any organization to apply the label 'Christian' to itself, this statement [Gaudium et spes No.76; ann. by the author] represents the only possible form for the Church to ask the pluralistic society to differentiate between what is Christian and what is not."[21] Confrontation with the other is mandatory; Jesus Christ himself was a great debater. Today it will not hurt either, if we engage in greater discussion. We need many more lively debates in order to walk together on the path of confrontation.

The strength of the flame

Christianity has become a minority religion in many Western countries. Although Christians are no longer the majority in a society, that does not mean, that they are alone. A Christian will never be alone. To be a Christian means to be under way with a community. And exactly in this community, that falters in the modern society, it is important to establish new and different values and at the same time to show a common flag, to keep the community from breaking apart. Even today a Christian community can still defend its special values and norms in society, and demonstrate that those values and norms are important.

This companionship differs from a political party, it is not a mere interest group. Rather it is driven by a spiritual force. Today, Christianity needs this force, which has helped the church to take new paths time and again in its history, more than ever it has helped to regard the gospel as more than a political program. The gospel represents a counter-project to the capitalistic system and neoliberals. It represents a contrast to our momentary dog-eat-dog society, where egotism, ruthlessness and violence dominate daily life.[22]

In Germany almost 60% of the population is still committed to a denomination. Many of the remaining 40% assume, that life becomes more simple without God and without belonging to a religious community. In modern times, the church needs Pentecostal tongues of fire which ignite the hearts of people. Passing on the flame keeps the fire burning. Currently there is a danger, at least in certain Western countries, that the church will allow the fire of faith to expire by degenerating into a bureaucratic apparatus. Church needs to be a fire for the people, a fire that gives warmth and comfort. To this end, it has to examine itself time and again, to make sure that it does not become lazy. For to start a fire and to keep it burning requires effort.

Everybody who burns for something can ignite somebody else. The Roman Catholic Church has got this special flame and the strength to inspire people. When people feel that flame burning inside themselves they succeed in inspiring their fellows.

A church that comes to the people

If people do not come to the church anymore, the church must come to the people.

In Bavaria there are Protestant priests who have converted shepherd's wagons into a mobile church and use those to visit the members of their parishes. To me this appears as a marvelous vehicle to enable the church to become flexible rather than always remain at the same location. Mass can be celebrated at all kinds of places, even in front of a shepherd's wagon under the open sky. The church has to be perpetually on its way to the people. Only by approaching people on the margins and caring for them can the church meet them in their concrete life situations and fulfill the task that Jesus Christ gave his disciples: "Go into all the world and preach the gospel to all creation" (Mark 16:15). Those who dare to go out and leave their home territory will have a better chance to be heard.

The road toward my destination

I am aware of the fact that I will have to go a long way towards the realization of my vocation. The goal is not yet within sight. Surely there will be lean periods and further obstacles ahead. However, so far, my faith has given me the strength to take this path. Even though not everybody likes to see me continue on the road towards the fulfillment of my vocation, it is still my path that I will follow.

I am being inconvenient to certain people now so that I will be able to live my vocation within the Roman Catholic Church in the future.

I will not hesitate or stop when faced with the opposition of reactionary bishops, clergy or laymen. I shall proceed on my way, in complete awareness, with full power and with the determination of my vocation.

When a few years ago I started to walk along the Way of St. James, I knew that there were would be several kilometers ahead of me. After the first day's march, I already realized that the next few days would not be easy. But I kept my destination in mind: Santiago de Compostela. On some days I felt that I was merely completing another leg of my journey. At other times, my feet hurt and my backpack seemed to be infinitely heavy. But I never had doubts about my goal. I clenched my teeth and continued to walk. I was optimistic that I would reach my destination. I have found that this kind of optimism as well as a certain assertiveness will help you to achieve your goals. I believe in the transformative power within the Roman Catholic

Church, a power caused and effected by the Holy Spirit. Therefore, I also believe that the Roman Catholic Church can indeed change and that it is worthwhile to walk new paths.

Summary

To be a provoker and let the Spirit of God guide us

To conclude, I would like to quote a saying of the South American liberation theologian Jon Sobrino who got to the very heart of what needs to be done now. He says that the church has to accept, "that God can still talk to us today, namely in the manner of the newness of God which cannot simply be deducted or extrapolated from what we know already about him. [...] This implies accepting our ignorance, in order to learn about God and about what his will is today."[23]

We do not know what is to come or which path the church will take in the future. God has already made possible quite a few changes during the history of the church. The Spirit of God blows where He wills. It will continue to act and cause effects in the future. For it is obvious that the Pope from Argentina has inspired the Roman Catholic Church with a new spirit. Perhaps I am a stumbling block and provoker, with my wish for and my ideas of a young, lively church, a church that lets women participate, a church for women and men equally. Basically, the words 'pro vocatio' mean a call for something. I challenge. I may be merely a young theologian on a long journey. But there is one clear objective in my mind: my vocation to be ordained as a priest in the Roman Catholic Church.

I trust that in the year 2040 that the structures of the church will be softer and more flexible. There will be married male and female priests, and homosexuals and divorcees will no longer be excluded from the sacraments. More people will be underway toward faith and will find a home within the church. This is my vision of the Roman Catholic Church. As this is what I wish for from the church, I will continue to stand up for the Roman Catholic Church and for my faith in God. The words of Marcus Tullius Cicero challenge me to continue to shape the vision of a new church, "Never begin to cease and never cease to begin". I will continue to work for the realization of an enlightened and unified church in the knowledge that everything is in God's hands.

Notes

1. see John A. Phillips: "Eve. The history of an idea", Harper & Row, 1984. or: http://godswordtowomen.org/eve_McNally.htm

2. Denise Buser: "The inequality is a consequence not of the act of ordination, but of the determination of the prerequisites that have to be fulfilled for ordination. Even if it is a consequence of can. 1024 CIC (Only a baptised male validly receives sacred ordination) that every Roman Catholic man (who so desires) is eligible for sacred ordination, the provision nonetheless specifies that an ordained person must be a man; therefore, women are excluded from ordination without exception and a priori." From this, Buser concluded, that females are discrimininated, because equal starting chances are not provided. see: Denise Buser: "Unholy Discrimination - An overview of the legal rules governing the consideration of the balance of interests between gender equality and the freedom of religion in access to leading spiritual offices", 11pp, 2015. https://ius.unibas.ch/fileadmin/user_upload/fe/file/UnholyDiscrimination_Englishedition.pdf

3. The apostolic letter "Ordinatio Sacerdotalis" (1994) not only stated, that priestly ordination is reserved for men alone, but also noticed, that this is "to be held always, everywhere, and by all, as belonging to the deposit of the faith". see: https://w2.vatican.va/content/john-paul ii/en/apost_letters/1994/documents/hf_jpii_apl_19940522_ordinatio-sacerdotalis.html and: "Responsum ad dubium concerning the teaching contained in 'Ordinatio

Sacerdotalis'", Congregation for the Doctrine of the Faith, 1995. From this it was concluded, that a ban on the discussion of female priesthood has been declared. G.L. Müller contradicted this conclusion, see G.L: Müller: "Hat die Kirche die Vollmacht, Frauen das Weihesakrament zu spenden?" (Is the Church allowed to administer the sacrament of Order to females?) in: Stimmen der Zeit 230: 173pp, 2012. "Even if the apostolic letter [here: Ordinatio Sacerdotalis] stated a ban on discussion of female priesthood, that would not be sustainable, since it contradicted the spirit of the second Vatican Council." see J.P. Neuner: "Zur ökumenischen Anerkennung kirchlicher Ämter." (Remarks on the ecumenical recognition of ecclesiastical positions) in: Stimmen der Zeit 232: 173pp, 2014.

4. see: Medard Kehl: "Die Kirche. Eine katholische Ekklesiologie." (The church: a Catholic ecclesiology) Echter, 1st edition, 1993, 457pp.

5. to list some of them: Ida Raming, Iris Müller, Elisabeth Schüssler Fiorenza, Gertrud Heinzelmann, Ute Eisen, Patricia Fresen, Arlene Swidler. Ida Raming, The Exclusion of Women from Priesthood: Divine Law or Sex Discrimination? The Scarecrow Press (Metuchen, N.J.) 1976. As well: Ida Raming, The Priestly Office of Women: God's Gift to a Renewed Church. The Scarecrow Press, Lanham; Maryland, 2004.

6. *Jesus Christ said: "I came not to send peace but a sword." (Matth 10:34).*

7. The old canon law from 1917 stated in Canon 1262: "It is to be desired that, in harmony with the ancient discipline of the Church, the women should in church be separated from the men. ... the women should assist in modest dress and with heads covered, especially when they approach the table of the Lord." see www. archive.org The new Canon Law: a commentary and summary of the new code of canon law, 1917.

8. see: Elisabeth Schüssler-Fiorenza In Memory of Her: "A Feminist Theological Reconstruction of Christian Origins", The Crossroad Publishing Company; 10th edition 1994. see: Ute E. Eisen: "Women

Officeholders in Early Christianity. Epigraphical and Literary Studies", Michael Glazier Books, 2000.

9. see Apostolic letter "Mulieris Dignitatem" of John Paul II. on the dignity and of women on the occasion of the Mariam year, see https://w2.vatican.va/content/john-paulii/en/apost_letters/1988.

10. Yves, Congar: "My Journal of the Council." English translation by Mary John Ronayne and Mary Cecily Boulding, Adelaide: ATF Theology, 2012.

11. see Encyclical letter "Lumen fidei" of the supreme pontiff Francis to the bishops priests and deacons consecrated persons and the lay faithful on faith, No. 4 from June 29, 2013. see https://w2.vatican.va.

12. see www.archive.org The new Canon Law: a commentary and summary of the new code of canon law, Canon 910 § 1, 1917.

13. see Franz-Josef Bode: "Als Mann und Frau schuf er sie. Über das Zusammenwirken von Frauen und Männern in der Kirche." (As male and female He created them. On the cooperation of women and men in the church.), Paderborn, 2013.

14. see https://www.opendoorsusa.org/christian-persecution.

15. "For it is the love of Christ which is moving us" (II Corinthians 5:14).

16. see Joseph Ratzinger: "Salt of the Earth: An Exclusive Interview on the State of the Church at the End of the Millennium", Ignatius Press, 1997.

17. see Dogmatic constitution on the church "Lumen Gentium", No.11: "Taking part in the Eucharistic sacrifice, which is the fount and apex of the whole Christian life..." November 21, 1964. see https:// www.vatican.va.

18. Friedrich Nietzsche: "Thus Spake Zarathustra: a Book for Everyone and No-one", see: "The Priests": " Better songs would they have to sing, for me to believe in their Saviour: more like saved ones would his disciples have to appear unto me!", http://www.

philosophy-index.com/nietzsche/thus-spake-zarathurstra/xxvi.php.

19. Apostolic Exhortation Evangelii Gaudium of the Holy Father Francis, see No.1 "The joy of the gospel". see https://www.vatican.va

20. see http://www.catholicnewsagency.com/news/vatican-stats-show-continued-growth-in-africa-asia/.

21. Karl Rahner, Herbert Vorgrimler: "Kleines Konzilskompendium" (Small compendium on the Council), 31st edition, Freiburg, p442, 1966. See: Herbert Vorgrimler, Commentary on the documents of Vatican II : Volume III., Bruns & Oates, 1979.

22. see Oswald von Nell-Breuning:"Kapitalismus-kritisch betrachtet. Zur Auseinandersetzung um das bessere ´System`" (Capitalism, viewed critically. On the controversy about the better ´system`), p38, Freiburg, 1974: "If one raises that kind of a capitalism to the status of a system with profit maximization as an axiom, then one makes abstract *acquisitiveness,* which in and by itself lacks any measure and therefore tends to excessively increase towards boundlessness, into an absolute principle. Such a ´system` would be inhuman."

23. Ignacio Ellacurie and Jon Sobrino (eds.): "Mysterium Liberationis: Fundamental Concepts of Liberation Theology." Chapter 30, "Communion, Conflict, and Ecclesial Solidarity", pp615, Orbis Books, 2004.

www.ingramcontent.com/pod-product-compliance
Lightning Source LLC
Chambersburg PA
CBHW050823090426
42738CB00020B/3467